YOUR KNOWLEDGE HAS VALUE

- We will publish your bachelor's and master's thesis, essays and papers
- Your own eBook and book - sold worldwide in all relevant shops
- Earn money with each sale

Upload your text at www.GRIN.com and publish for free

Nitin Chikani

HTML & Advanced HTML Programming for Beginners

GRIN Verlag

Bibliografische Information der Deutschen Nationalbibliothek:

Die Deutsche Bibliothek verzeichnet diese Publikation in der Deutschen Nationalbibliografie; detaillierte bibliografische Daten sind im Internet über http://dnb.d-nb.de/ abrufbar.

Imprint:

Druck und Bindung: Books on Demand GmbH, Norderstedt Germany
ISBN: 978-3-656-60752-6

This book at GRIN:

http://www.grin.com/en/e-book/269212/html-advanced-html-programming-for-beginners

GRIN - Your knowledge has value

Der GRIN Verlag publiziert seit 1998 wissenschaftliche Arbeiten von Studenten, Hochschullehrern und anderen Akademikern als eBook und gedrucktes Buch. Die Verlagswebsite www.grin.com ist die ideale Plattform zur Veröffentlichung von Hausarbeiten, Abschlussarbeiten, wissenschaftlichen Aufsätzen, Dissertationen und Fachbüchern.

Visit us on the internet:

http://www.grin.com/

http://www.facebook.com/grincom

http://www.twitter.com/grin_com

- **Introduction to HTML**

- Webpages are written in HTML - a simple scripting language.
- HTML is short for HyperText Markup Language.
- Hypertext is simply a piece of text that works as a link.
- Markup Language is a way of writing layout information within documents.
- Basically an HTML document is a plain text file that contains text and nothing else.
- When a browser opens an HTML file, the browser will look for HTML codes in the text and use them to change the layout, insert images, or create links to other pages.
- Since HTML documents are just text files they can be written in even the simplest text editor.
- A more popular choice is to use a special HTML editor - maybe even one that puts focus on the visual result rather than the codes - a so-called WYSIWYG editor ("What You See Is What You Get").
- Some of the most popular HTML editors, such as FrontPage or Dreamweaver will let you create pages more or less as you write documents in Word or whatever text editor you're using.
- However, there are some very good reasons to create your own pages - or parts of them - by hand...

- **Introduction Advanced HTML 5.**

- HTML5 will be the new standard for HTML.
- The previous version of HTML, HTML 4.01, came in 1999. The internet has changed significantly since then.
- HTML5 is intended to subsume not only HTML 4, but also XHTML 1 and DOM Level 2 HTML.

- HTML5 is designed to deliver almost everything you want to do online without requiring additional plugins. It does everything from animation to apps, music to movies, and can also be used to build complicated applications that run in your browser.
- HTML5 is also cross-platform (it does not care whether you are using a tablet or a smartphone, a netbook, notebook or a Smart TV).
- HTML5 can also be used to write web applications that still work when you are not online.
- The HTML 5 working group includes AOL, Apple, Google, IBM, Microsoft, Mozilla, Nokia, Opera, and hundreds of other vendors.
- HTML5 is still a work in progress. However, all major browsers support many of the new HTML5 elements and APIs.

✓ **Some rules for HTML5 were established:**

- New features should be based on HTML, CSS, DOM, and JavaScript
- The need for external plugins (like Flash) needs to be reduced
- Error handling should be easier than in previous versions
- Scripting has to be replaced by more markup
- HTML5 should be device-independent
- The development process should be visible to the public

Prog.1 Example for Heading and Paragraph.

```
<html>
<body>
        <h1>Prof. Nitin Chikani</h1>
        <p>My first paragraph. </p>
</body>
</html>
```

Output:

Prof. Nitin Chikani

My first paragraph.

Prog. 2 Example for Multiple Heading.

```
<html>
<body>
        <h1>This is First heading </h1>
        <h2>This is Second heading </h2>
        <h3>This is Third heading </h3>
        <h4>This is Fourth heading </h4>
        <h5>This is Five heading </h5>
        <h6>This is Six heading </h6>
</body>
</html>
```

Output:

This is First heading

This is Second heading

This is Third heading

This is Fourth heading

This is Five heading

This is Six heading

Prog. 3 Example for Linking page.

```
<html>
<body>
        <a href="http://www.techsinformation.com">
          This is a link</a>
</body>
</html>
```

Output:

This is a link

Prog. 4 Example for Print Horizontal line in HTML.

```
<html>
<body>
        <p>The hr tag defines a horizontal rule:</p>
        <hr>
                <p>This is a First paragraph.</p>
        <hr>
                <p>This is a Second paragraph.</p>
        <hr>
```

```
        <p>This is a Third paragraph.</p>
</body>
</html>
```

Output:

The hr tag defines a horizontal rule:

This is a First paragraph.

This is a Second paragraph.

This is a Third paragraph.

Prog. 5 Example for Print Multiple Paragraph in HTML.

```
<html>
<body>
    <p>
        This paragraph
        contains a lot of lines
        in the source code,
        but the browser
        ignores it.
    </p>
    <p>
        This paragraph
        contains      a lot of spaces
        in the source      code,
        but the     browser
```

```
        ignores it.
    </p>
    <p>
The number of lines in a paragraph depends on the size of your browser window. If you resize the browser window, the number of lines in this paragraph will change.
    </p>
</body>
</html>
```

Output:

This paragraph contains a lot of lines in the source code, but the browser ignores it.

This paragraph contains a lot of spaces in the source code, but the browser ignores it.

The number of lines in a paragraph depends on the size of your browser window. If you resize the browser window, the number of lines in this paragraph will change.

Prog. 6 Example for line break in paragraph.

```
<html>
<body>
    <p>This is<br>a para<br>graph with line breaks</p>
</body>
</html>
```

Output:

This is
a para
graph with line breaks

Prog. 7 Example for multiple text formatting in HTML.

```
<html>
```


Prof. Nitin Chikani
Atmiya Institute Of Technology & Sci. Rajkot, India

```
<body>
        <p><b>This text is bold</b></p>
        <p><strong>This text is good</strong></p>
        <p><em>This text is emphasized</em></p>
        <p><i>This text is italic</i></p>
        <p><small>This text is very small</small></p>
        <p>This is<sub> subscript</sub> and <sup>superscript</sup></p>
</body>
</html>
```

Output:

This text is bold

This text is good

This text is emphasized

This text is italic

This text is very small

This is $_{\text{subscript}}$ and ^{superscript}

Prog. 8 Example for control line breaks and spaces in HTML.

```
<html>
<body>
        <pre>
                This is
                preformatted text.
                It preserves      both spaces
                and line breaks.
        </pre>
```


Prof. Nitin Chikani
Atmiya Institute Of Technology & Sci. Rajkot, India

```
        <p>The pre tag is good for displaying computer code:</p>
        <pre>
                for i = 1 to 10
                print i
                next i
        </pre>
</body>
</html>
```

Output:

```
This is
preformatted text.
It preserves      both spaces
and line breaks.
```

The pre tag is good for displaying computer code:

```
for i = 1 to 10
    print i
next i
```

Prog. 9 Example for Different Computer Output tags.

```
<html>
<body>
<code>Computer code</code>
        <br>
                <kbd>Keyboard input</kbd>
        <br>
                <samp>Sample text</samp>
        <br>
                <var>Computer variable</var>
        <br>
```


Prof. Nitin Chikani
Atmiya Institute Of Technology & Sci. Rajkot, India

```
        <p><b>Note:</b> These tags are often used to display
        computer/programming code.</p>
</body>
</html>
```

Output:

```
Computer code
Keyboard input
Sample text
```
Computer variable

Note: These tags are often used to display computer/programming code.

Prog. 10 Example for Insert Contact Information in HTML.

```
<html>
<body>
<address>
    Written by Prof. Nitin Chikani<br>
    <a href="www.techsinformation.com">Email us</a><br>
    Address: Box 564, India<br>
    Phone: +12 34 56 78
</address>
</body></html>
```

Output:

Written by Prof. Nitin Chikani
Email us
Address: Box 564, India
Phone: +12 34 56 78

Prog. 11 Example for Abbreviations and Acronyms in HTML.

```
<html>
<body>
        <p>The <abbr title="Nitiin Parshotambhai Chikani">NPC</abbr> was born in
            1984.
        </p>
        <p>Can I get this <abbr title="as soon as possible">ASAP</abbr>?</p>
        <p>the title attribute is used to show the spelled-out version when holding the
            mouse pointer over The acronym or abbreviation. </p>
</body>
</html>
```

Output:

The NPC was born in 1984.

Can I get this ASAP?

The title attribute is used to show the spelled-out version when holding the mouse pointer over the acronym or abbreviation.

Prog. 12 Example for mark deleted and inserted text in HTML.

```
<html>
<body>
        <p>My favorite color is <del>black</del> <ins>pink</ins>!</p>
        <p>Notice that browsers will strikethrough deleted text and underline inserted
            text.</p>
</body>
</html>
```

Output:

Prof. Nitin Chikani
Atmiya Institute Of Technology & Sci. Rajkot, India

My favorite color is ~~black~~ pink!

Notice that browsers will strikethrough deleted text and underline inserted text.

Prog. 13 Example for Style HTML Elements.

```
<html>
<body>
    <div
    style="opacity:0.5;position:absolute;left:50px;width:300px;height:150px;backgro
    und-color:#40B3DF">
    </div>
    <div style="font-family:verdana;padding:20px;border-radius:10px;border:10px
    solid #EE872A;">
    <div
    style="opacity:0.3;position:absolute;left:120px;width:100px;height:200px;backgr
    ound-color:#8AC007"></div>
    <h3>Look! Styles and colors</h3>
    <div style="letter-spacing:12px;">Manipulate Text</div>
    <div style="color:#40B3DF;">Colors
    <span style="background-color:#B4009E;color:#ffffff;">Boxes</span>
    </div>
    <div style="color:#000000;">and more...</div>
    </div>
</body>
</html>
```

Output:

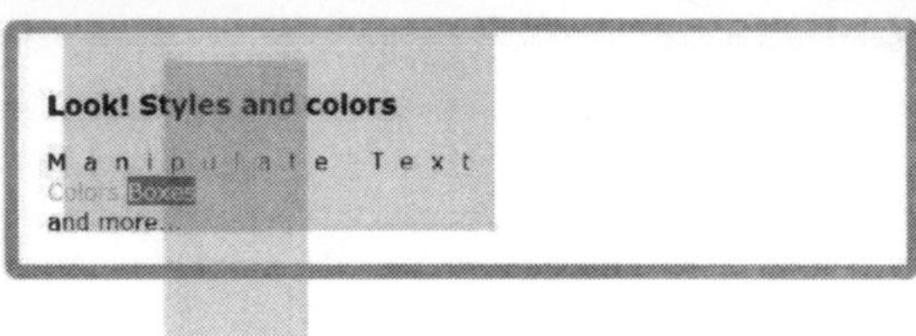

Prog. 14 Example for Background color in HTML.

```
<html>
<body style="background-color:yellow;">
        <h2 style="background-color:red;">This is a heading</h2>
        <p style="background-color:green;">This is a paragraph.</p>
</body></html>
```

Output:

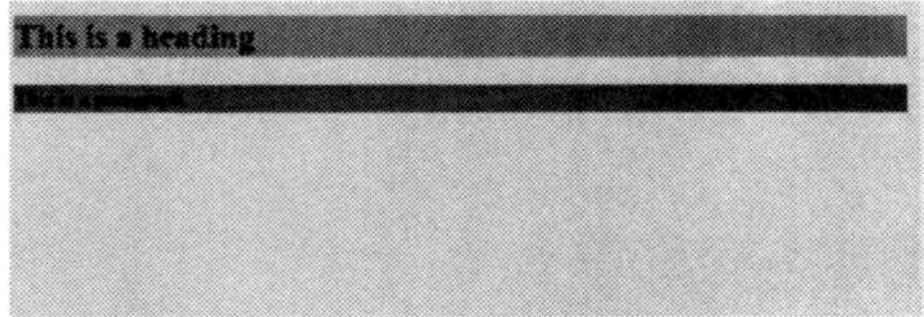

Prog. 15 Example for Style color, font and size in HTML.

```
<html>
<body>
        <h1 style="font-family:verdana;">its Rocking</h1>
        <p style="font-family:arial;color:red;font-size:20px;">A paragraph.</p>
</body>
</html>
```

Output:

its Rocking

A paragraph.

Prog. 16 Example for center alignment text in HTML.

```
<html>
<body>
        <h1 style="text-align:center;">Center-aligned heading</h1>
        <p>This is a paragraph.</p>
        <p> hi everyone</p>
        <p> we are best</p>
</body>
</html>
```

Output:

Center-aligned heading

This is a paragraph.

hi everyone

we are best

Prog. 17 Example for set the font, font-size and font color of text in HTML.

```
<html>
<body>
        <p style="font-family:arial;font-size:110%;color:red">
        This is a paragraph with some text in it. This is a paragraph with some text in it.
        This is a paragraph with some text in it. This is a paragraph with some text in it.
        </p>
```


Prof. Nitin Chikani
Atmiya Institute Of Technology & Sci. Rajkot, India

```
</body>
</html>
```

Output:

This is a paragraph with some text in it. This is a paragraph with some text in it. This is a paragraph with some text in it. This is a paragraph with some text in it.

Prog. 18 Example for set external style sheet using HTML.

```
<html>
<head>
        <link rel="stylesheet" type="text/css" href="styles.css">
        </head>
        <body>
        <h1>I am formatted with an external style sheet</h1>
        <p>Me too!</p>
</body>
</html>
```

Output:

I am formatted with an external style sheet

Me too!

Prog. 19 Example for create Hyperlink in HTML.

```
<html>
<body>
        <p>
        <a href="http://npchikani.wordpress.com">wordpress blog</a> This is a link to a
        page on this website.
```


Prof. Nitin Chikani
Atmiya Institute Of Technology & Sci. Rajkot, India

```
        </p>
        <p>
        <a href="http://www.techsinformation.com/">techsinformation</a> This is a link
        to a website on the World Wide Web.
        </p>
</body>
</html>
```

Output:

wordpress blog This is a link to a page on this website.

techsinformation This is a link to a website on the World Wide Web.

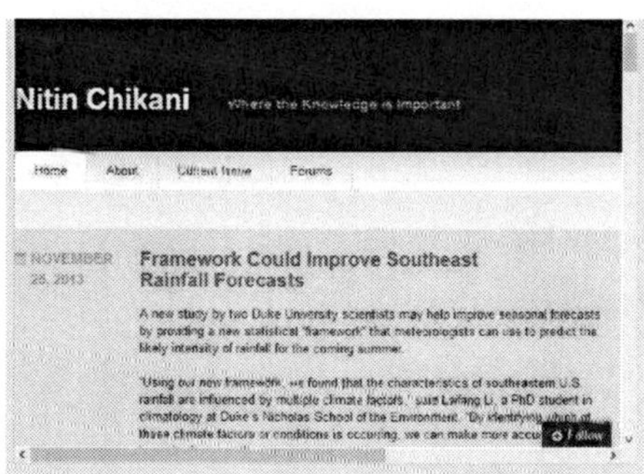

Prog. 20 Example for how to give image link in HTML.

```
<html>
<body>
        <p>Create a link of an image:
        <a href="http://www.techsinformation.com">
        <img src="smiley.gif" alt="HTML tutorial" width="42" height="42"></a></p>
        <p>No border around the image, but still a link:
```

```
    <a href="http://www.techsinformation.com">
    <img style="border:0;" src="smiley.gif" alt="HTML tutorial" width="42"
    height="42"></a></p>
</body>
</html>
```

Output:

Create a link of an image:

No border around the image, but still a link: 

Prog. 21 Example for open new browser window in HTML.

```
<html>
<body>
    <a href="http://www.techsinformation.com" target="_blank">
    Visit techsinformation.com!</a>
    <p>If you set the target attribute to "_blank", the link will open in a new browser
    window/tab.</p>
</body>
</html>
```

Output:

Visit techsinformation.com!

If you set the target attribute to "_blank", the link will open in a new browser window/tab.

Prog. 22 Example for Insert image in HTML.

```
<html>
<body>
        <p>
        An image:
        <img src="smiley.gif" alt="Smiley face" width="42" height="42"></p>
        <p>
        A moving image:
        <img src="hackanm.gif" alt="Computer man" width="48" height="48"></p>
        <p>
        Note that the syntax of inserting a moving image is no different from a non-
        moving image.
        </p>
</body>
</html>
```

Output:

Note that the syntax of inserting a moving image is no different from a non-moving image.

Prog. 23 Example for create an image map with clickable region in HTML.

```
<html>
<body>
        <p>Click on the sun or on one of the planets to watch it closer:</p>
```


Prof. Nitin Chikani
Atmiya Institute Of Technology & Sci. Rajkot, India

```
        <img src="planets.gif" width="145" height="126" alt="Planets"
        usemap="#planetmap">
        <map name="planetmap">
          <area shape="rect" coords="0,0,82,126" alt="Sun" href="sun.htm">
          <area shape="circle" coords="90,58,3" alt="Mercury" href="mercur.htm">
          <area shape="circle" coords="124,58,8" alt="Venus" href="venus.htm">
        </map>
</body>
</html>
```

Output:

Click on the sun or on one of the planets to watch it closer:

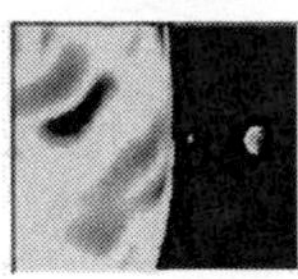

Prog.24 Example for create table with boarder in HTML.

```
<html>
<body>
        <p>
        Each table starts with a table tag.
        Each table row starts with a tr tag.
        Each table data starts with a td tag.
        </p>
        <h4>One column:</h4>
        <table border="2">
        <tr>
```


Prof. Nitin Chikani
Atmiya Institute Of Technology & Sci. Rajkot, India

```
<td>1000</td>
</tr>
</table>
<h4>One row and three columns:</h4>
<table border="1">
<tr>
  <td>1000</td>
  <td>2000</td>
  <td>3000</td>
</tr>
</table>
<h4>Two rows and three columns:</h4>
<table border="1">
<tr>
  <td>1000</td>
  <td>2000</td>
  <td>3000</td>
</tr>
<tr>
  <td>4000</td>
  <td>5000</td>
  <td>6000</td>
</tr>
</table></body></html>
```

Output:

Prof. Nitin Chikani
Atmiya Institute Of Technology & Sci. Rajkot, India

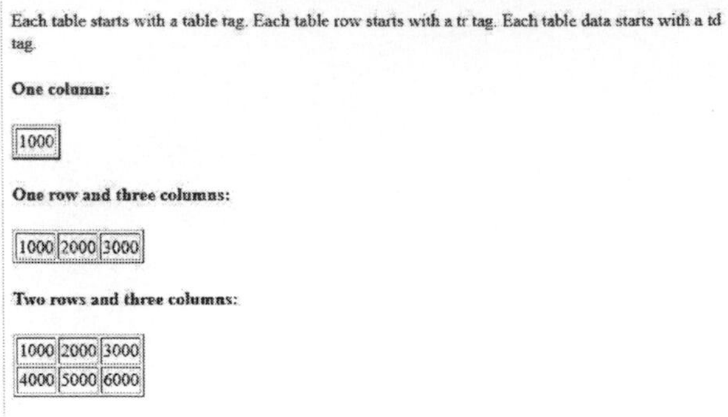

Each table starts with a table tag. Each table row starts with a tr tag. Each table data starts with a td tag.

One column:

1000

One row and three columns:

1000	2000	3000

Two rows and three columns:

1000	2000	3000
4000	5000	6000

Prog. 25 Example for create table without boarder in HTML.

```
<html>
<body>
        <h4>This table has no borders:</h4>
        <table>
        <tr>
          <td>1000</td>
          <td>2000</td>
          <td>3000</td>
        </tr>
        <tr>
          <td>4000</td>
          <td>5000</td>
          <td>6000</td>
        </tr>
        </table>
        <h4>And this table has no borders:</h4>
        <table border="0">
```

```
        <tr>
          <td>1000</td>
          <td>2000</td>
          <td>3000</td>
        </tr>
        <tr>
          <td>4000</td>
          <td>5000</td>
          <td>6000</td>
        </tr>
        </table>
</body>
</html>
```

Output:

This table has no borders:

1000 2000 3000
4000 5000 6000

And this table has no borders:

1000 2000 3000
4000 5000 6000

Prog. 26 Example for create table with header in HTML.

```
<html>
<body>
        <h4>Table headers:</h4>
        <table border="1">
        <tr>
```


Prof. Nitin Chikani
Atmiya Institute Of Technology & Sci. Rajkot, India

```
  <th>Name</th>
  <th>Telephone</th>
  <th>Telephone</th>
</tr>
<tr>
  <td>Bill Gates</td>
  <td>5252 77 854</td>
  <td>5252 77 855</td>
</tr>
</table>
<h4>Vertical headers:</h4>
<table border="1">
<tr>
  <th>First Name:</th>
  <td>Bill Gates</td>
</tr>
<tr>
  <th>Telephone:</th>
  <td>5252 77 854</td>
</tr>
<tr>
  <th>Telephone:</th>
  <td>5252 77 855</td>
</tr>
</table>
</body>
```


Prof. Nitin Chikani
Atmiya Institute Of Technology & Sci. Rajkot, India

```
</html>
```

Output:

Table headers:

Name	Telephone	Telephone
Bill Gates	5252 77 854	5252 77 855

Vertical headers:

First Name:	Bill Gates
Telephone:	5252 77 854
Telephone:	5252 77 855

Prog. 27 Example for create table cells that span more than one row/ column.

```
<html>
<body>
        <h4>Cell that spans two columns:</h4>
        <table border="1">
        <tr>
          <th>Name</th>
          <th colspan="2">Telephone</th>
        </tr>
        <tr>
          <td>Bill Gates</td>
          <td>5252 77 854</td>
          <td>5252 77 855</td>
        </tr>
        </table>
        <h4>Cell that spans two rows:</h4>
```

```
<table border="1">
<tr>
  <th>First Name:</th>
  <td>Bill Gates</td>
</tr>
<tr>
  <th rowspan="2">Telephone:</th>
  <td>5252 77 854</td>
</tr>
<tr>
  <td>5252 77 855</td>
</tr>
</table>
</body>
</html>
```

Output:

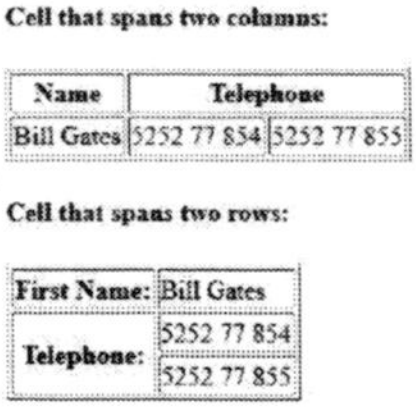

Cell that spans two columns:

Name	Telephone	
Bill Gates	5252 77 854	5252 77 855

Cell that spans two rows:

First Name:	Bill Gates
Telephone:	5252 77 854
	5252 77 855

Prog. 28 Example for control white space between cell content and boarder in HTML.

```
<html>
<body>
```

```
        <h4>Without cellpadding:</h4>
        <table border="1">
                <tr>
                  <td>First</td>
                  <td>Row</td>
                </tr>
                <tr>
                  <td>Second</td>
                  <td>Row</td>
                </tr>
        </table>
        <h4>With cellpadding:</h4>
        <table border="1" cellpadding="10">
                <tr>
                  <td>First</td>
                  <td>Row</td>
                </tr>
                <tr>
                  <td>Second</td>
                  <td>Row</td>
                </tr>
        </table>
</body>
</html>
```

Output:

Prof. Nitin Chikani
Atmiya Institute Of Technology & Sci. Rajkot, India

Without cellpadding:

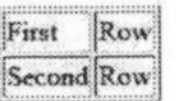

First	Row
Second	Row

With cellpadding:

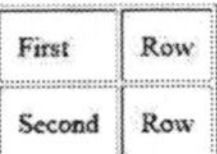

First	Row
Second	Row

Prog. 29 Example for Different types of Ordered list in HTML.

```
<html>
<body>
        <h4>Numbered list:</h4>
        <ol>
         <li>Nitin</li>
         <li>Mayur</li>
         <li>Jayesh</li>
         <li>Rajesh</li>
        </ol>
        <h4>Letters list:</h4>
        <ol type="A">
         <li>Nitin</li>
         <li>Mayur</li>
         <li>Jayesh</li>
         <li>Rajesh</li>
        </ol>
        <h4>Lowercase letters list:</h4>
        <ol type="a">
         <li>Nitin</li>
```

```
    <li>Mayur</li>
    <li>Jayesh</li>
    <li>Rajesh</li>
   </ol>
   <h4>Roman numbers list:</h4>
   <ol type="I">
    <li>Nitin</li>
    <li>Mayur</li>
    <li>Jayesh</li>
    <li>Rajesh</li>
   </ol>
   <h4>Lowercase Roman numbers list:</h4>
   <ol type="i">
    <li>Nitin</li>
    <li>MAyur</li>
    <li>Jayesh</li>
    <li>Rajesh</li>
   </ol>
</body>
</html>
```

Output:

Prof. Nitin Chikani
Atmiya Institute Of Technology & Sci. Rajkot, India

Numbered list:

1. Nitin
2. Mayur
3. Jayesh
4. Rajesh

Letters list:

A. Nitin
B. Mayur
C. Jayesh
D. Rajesh

Lowercase letters list:

a. Nitin
b. Mayur
c. Jayesh
d. Rajesh

Roman numbers list:

Roman numbers list:

I. Nitin
II. Mayur
III. Jayesh
IV. Rajesh

Lowercase Roman numbers list:

i. Nitin
ii. MAyur
iii. Jayesh
iv. Rajesh

Prog. 30 Example for different type's unordered list in HTML.

```
<html>
<body>
        <h4>Disc bullets list:</h4>
        <ul style="list-style-type:disc">
         <li>Nitin</li>
         <li>Mayur</li>
         <li>Jayesh</li>
         <li>Rajesh</li>
        </ul>
        <h4>Circle bullets list:</h4>
        <ul style="list-style-type:circle">
         <li>Nitin</li>
         <li>Mayur</li>
         <li>Jayesh</li>
         <li>Rajesh</li>
```


Prof. Nitin Chikani
Atmiya Institute Of Technology & Sci. Rajkot, India

```
    </ul>
    <h4>Square bullets list:</h4>
    <ul style="list-style-type:square">
     <li>Nitin</li>
     <li>Mayur</li>
     <li>Jayesh</li>
     <li>Rajesh</li>
    </ul>
    <p><b>Note:</b> The type attribute of the ul tag is deprecated in HTML 4, and
    is not supported in HTML5.Therefore we have used the style attribute and the
    CSS list-style-type property, to define different types of unordered lists
    below:</p>
</body>
</html>
```

Output:

Disc bullets list:

- Nitin
- Mayur
- Jayesh
- Rajesh

Circle bullets list:

- Nitin
- Mayur
- Jayesh
- Rajesh

Square bullets list:

- Nitin
- Mayur
- Jayesh
- Rajesh

Prog. 31 Example for create multiple nested list in HTML.

```
<html>
<body>
        <h4>A nested List:</h4>
        <ul>
          <li>Coffee</li>
          <li>Tea
            <ul>
            <li>Black tea</li>
            <li>Green tea
              <ul>
              <li>China</li>
              <li>Africa</li>
              </ul>
            </li>
         </ul>
         </li>
         <li>Milk</li>
        </ul>
</body>
</html>
```

Output:

Prof. Nitin Chikani
Atmiya Institute Of Technology & Sci. Rajkot, India

A nested List:

- Coffee
- Tea
  - Black tea
  - Green tea
    - China
    - Africa
- Milk

Prog. 32 Example for Input field text and password in HTML.

```
<html>
<body>
        <form action="">
        First name:       <input type="text" name="firstname"><br>
        Last name:        <input type="text" name="lastname"><br>
        Password:         <input type="password" name="password"><br>
        Re-Type Password: <input type="password" name="password">
        </form>
        <p><b>Note :< /b> the form itself is not visible. Also note that the default width
        of a text field is 20 characters. </p>
</body>
</html>
```

Output:

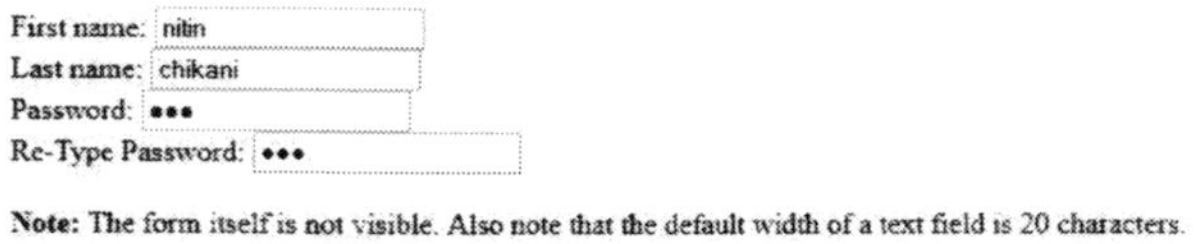

First name: nitin
Last name: chikani
Password: •••
Re-Type Password: •••

Note: The form itself is not visible. Also note that the default width of a text field is 20 characters.

Prog. 33 Example for create checkbox and radio button in HTML.

```
<html>
<body>
        <form action="">
        <input type="checkbox" name="vehicle" value="Bike">I have a bike<br>
        <input type="checkbox" name="vehicle" value="Car">I have a car<br>
        <input type="radio" name="sex" value="male">Male<br>
        <input type="radio" name="sex" value="female">Female<br>
        <input type="button" value="Hello world!">
        </form>
</body>
</html>
```

Output:

I have a bike
I have a car
Male
Female
Hello world!

Prog. 34 Example for create multiple drop down list with selected value in HTML.

```
<html>
<body>
        <form action="">
        <select name="cars">
        <option value="volvo">Volvo</option>
        <option value="saab">Saab</option>
        <option value="fiat" selected>Fiat</option>
        <option value="audi">Audi</option>
```

```
        </select>
        </form>
</body>
</html>
```

Output:

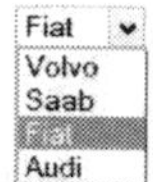

Prog. 35 Example for Create textarea in HTML.

```
<html>
<body>
        <textarea rows="5" cols="20">
        The girl was playing in the garden.
        </textarea>
</body>
</html>
```

Output:

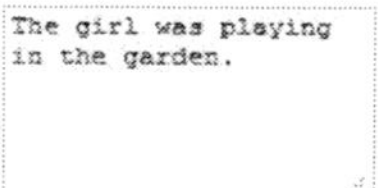

Prog. 36 Example for Input value into text and display value in action page.

```
<html>
<body>
        <form name="input" action="html_form_action.html" method="get">
        First name: <input type="text" name="FirstName" value="Nitin"><br>
```


Prof. Nitin Chikani
Atmiya Institute Of Technology & Sci. Rajkot, India

```
        Last name: <input type="text" name="LastName" value="Chikani"><br>
        <input type="submit" value="Submit">
        </form>
        <p>If you click the "Submit" button, the form-data will be sent to a page called
        "html_form_action.html". </p>
</body>
</html>
```

Output:

First name: Nitin
Last name: Chikani
Submit

If you click the "Submit" button, the form-data will be sent to a page called "html_form_action.html".

Prog. 37 Example for select value using checkbox and display in action page.

```
<html>
<body>
        <form name="input" action="html_form_action.html" method="get">
        <input type="checkbox" name="vehicle" value="Bike">I have a sportbike<br>
        <input type="checkbox" name="vehicle" value="Car">I have a sportcar
        <br><br>
        <input type="submit" value="Submit">
        </form>
        <p>if you click the "Submit" button, the form-data will be sent to a page called
        "html_form_action.html". </p>
</body>
</html>
```

Output:

☑ I have a sportbike
☑ I have a sportcar

Submit

If you click the "Submit" button, the form-data will be sent to a page called "html_form_action.html".

Prog. 38 Example for select value using radio and display in action page.

```
<html>
<body>
        <form name="input" action="html_form_action.html" method="get">
        <input type="radio" name="sex" value="male">Male<br>
        <input type="radio" name="sex" value="female">Female<br>
        <input type="submit" value="Submit">
        </form>
        <p>If you click the "Submit" button, the form-data will be sent to a page called
        "html_form_action.html". </p>
</body>
</html>
```

Output:

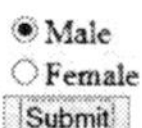

If you click the "Submit" button, the form-data will be sent to a page called "html_form_action.html".

Prog. 39 Example for send mail to someone in HTML.

```
<html>
<body>
        <h3>Send e-mail to someone@example.com:</h3>
```

```
    <form action="MAILTO:someone@example.com" method="post"
    enctype="text/plain">
    Name:<br>
    <input type="text" name="name" value="Enter your name"><br>
    E-mail:<br>
    <input type="text" name="mail" value="Enter your email"><br>
    Comment:<br>
    <input type="text" name="comment" value="Enter your comment"
    size="50"><br><br>
    <input type="submit" value="Send">
    <input type="reset" value="Reset">
    </form>
</body>
</html>
```

Output:

Send e-mail to someone@example.com:

Name:
Enter your name
E-mail:
Enter your email
Comment:
Enter your comment

Send Reset

Prog. 40 Example for create metadata in heading section in HTML.

```
<html>
<head>
<meta name="description" content="Free Web tutorials">
<meta name="keywords" content="HTML,CSS,XML,JavaScript">
```


Prof. Nitin Chikani
Atmiya Institute Of Technology & Sci. Rajkot, India

```
<meta name="author" content="Hege Refsnes">
<meta charset="UTF-8">
</head>
<body>
	<p>All meta information goes in the head section...</p>
</body>
</html>
```

Output:

All meta information goes in the head section...

Prog. 41 Example for writing script in HTML.

```
<html>
<body>
<script>
		document.write("Hi everyone!")
		document.write("We Are Best")
</script>
</body>
</html>
```

Output:

Hi everyone!We Are Best

Prof. Nitin Chikani
Atmiya Institute Of Technology & Sci. Rajkot, India

Advanced HTML5 New Elements

- **New Elements in HTML5**

- The internet, and the use of the internet, has changed a lot since HTML 4.01 became a standard in 1999.
- Today, several elements in HTML 4.01 are obsolete, never used, or not used the way they were intended. All those elements are removed or re-written in HTML5.
- To better handle today's internet use, HTML5 also includes new elements for drawing graphics, adding media content, better page structure, better form handling, and several APIs to drag/drop elements, find Geolocation, include web storage, application cache, web workers, etc.

1. **The New <canvas> Element**

- The <canvas> tag is only a container for graphics, you must use a script to actually draw the graphics.

Example:

```
<html>
<body>
        <canvas id="myCanvas">Your browser does not support the HTML5 canvas
        tag.</canvas>
        <script>
        var c=document.getElementById('myCanvas');
        var ctx=c.getContext('2d');
        ctx.fillStyle='#FF0000';
        ctx.fillRect(0,0,80,100);
        </script>
</body>
```

</html>

Output:

2. New Media Elements

Tag	Description
<audio>	Defines sound content
<video>	Defines a video or movie
<source>	Defines multiple media resources for <video> and <audio>
<embed>	Defines a container for an external application or interactive content (a plug-in)
<track>	Defines text tracks for <video> and <audio>

2.1 <audio> Tag

❖ **Definition and Usage and supported format.**

➢ The <audio> tag defines sound, such as music or other audio streams.
Currently, there are 3 supported file formats for the <audio> element:
MP3, Wav, and Ogg:

Prof. Nitin Chikani
Atmiya Institute Of Technology & Sci. Rajkot, India

Browser	MP3	Wav	Ogg
Internet Explorer	YES	NO	NO
Chrome	YES	YES	YES
Firefox	NO **Update:** Firefox 21 running on Windows 7, Windows 8, Windows Vista, and Android now supports MP3	YES	YES
Safari	YES	YES	NO
Opera	NO	YES	YES

MIME Types for Audio Formats

Format	MIME-type
MP3	audio/mpeg
Ogg	audio/ogg
Wav	audio/wav

❖ Attributes new in HTML5.

Attributes

New : New in HTML5.

Attribute		Value	Description
autoplay	New	autoplay	Specifies that the audio will start playing as soon as it is ready
controls	New	controls	Specifies that audio controls should be displayed (such as a play/pause button etc).
loop	New	loop	Specifies that the audio will start over again, every time it is finished
muted	New	muted	Specifies that the audio output should be muted
preload	New	auto metadata none	Specifies if and how the author thinks the audio should be loaded when the page loads
src	New	*URL*	Specifies the URL of the audio file

Example:

```
<html>
<body>
        <audio controls>
          <source src="horse.ogg" type="audio/ogg">
          <source src="horse.mp3" type="audio/mpeg">
```

```
    </audio>
</body>
</html>
```

Output:

2.2<video> tag

❖ **Definition and Usage**

➢ The <video> tag specifies video, such as a movie clip or other video streams. Currently, there are 3 supported video formats for the <video> element: MP4, WebM, and Ogg:

Browser	MP4	WebM	Ogg
Internet Explorer	YES	NO	NO
Chrome	YES	YES	YES
Firefox	NO **Update:** Firefox 21 running on Windows 7, Windows 8, Windows Vista, and Android now supports MP4	YES	YES
Safari	YES	NO	NO
Opera	NO	YES	YES

- MP4 = MPEG 4 files with H264 video codec and AAC audio codec
- WebM = WebM files with VP8 video codec and Vorbis audio codec
- Ogg = Ogg files with Theora video codec and Vorbis audio codec

MIME Types for Video Formats

Format	MIME-type
MP4	video/mp4
WebM	video/webm
Ogg	video/ogg

Prof. Nitin Chikani
Atmiya Institute Of Technology & Sci. Rajkot, India

❖ Optional Attributes

New : New in HTML5.

Attribute		Value	Description
autoplay	New	autoplay	Specifies that the video will start playing as soon as it is ready
controls	New	controls	Specifies that video controls should be displayed (such as a play/pause button etc).
height	New	*pixels*	Sets the height of the video player
loop	New	loop	Specifies that the video will start over again, every time it is finished
muted	New	muted	Specifies that the audio output of the video should be muted
poster	New	*URL*	Specifies an image to be shown while the video is downloading, or until the user hits the play button
preload	New	auto metadata none	Specifies if and how the author thinks the video should be loaded when the page loads
src	New	*URL*	Specifies the URL of the video file
width	New	*pixels*	Sets the width of the video player

Example:

```
<html>
<body>
        <video width="320" height="240" controls>
          <source src="movie.mp4" type="video/mp4">
          <source src="movie.ogg" type="video/ogg">
          Your browser does not support the video tag.
        </video>
</body>
</html>
```

Output:

2.3<source> tag

❖ **Definition and Usage**

➢ The <source> tag is used to specify multiple media resources for media elements, such as <video> and <audio>.

➢ The <source> tag allows you to specify alternative video/audio files which the browser may choose from, based on its media type or codec support.

❖ **Attributes:**

New : New in HTML5.

Attribute		Value	Description
media	New	*media_query*	Specifies the type of media resource
src	New	*URL*	Specifies the URL of the media file
type	New	*MIME_type*	Specifies the MIME type of the media resource

Example:

```
<html>
<body>
        <audio controls>
        <source src="horse.ogg" type="audio/ogg">
        <source src="horse.mp3" type="audio/mpeg">
```


Prof. Nitin Chikani
Atmiya Institute Of Technology & Sci. Rajkot, India

Your browser does not support the audio element.

</audio>

</body>

</html>

Output:

2.4 <embed> tag

❖ **Definition and Usage**

➢ The <embed> tag defines a container for an external application or interactive content (a plug-in).

❖ **Attributes:**

New : New in HTML5.

Attribute		Value	Description
height	New	*pixels*	Specifies the height of the embedded content
src	New	*URL*	Specifies the address of the external file to embed
type	New	*MIME_type*	Specifies the MIME type of the embedded content
width	New	*pixels*	Specifies the width of the embedded content

Example:

```
<html>
<body>
    <embed src="helloworld.swf">
</body>
</html>
```

Output:

Prof. Nitin Chikani
Atmiya Institute Of Technology & Sci. Rajkot, India

Hel... World!

2.5<track> tag

❖ **Definition and Usage**

- The <track> tag specifies text tracks for media elements (<audio> and <video>).
- This element is used to specify subtitles, caption files or other files containing text that should be visible when the media is playing.

❖ **Optional Attributes:**

New : New in HTML5.

Attribute		Value	Description
default	New	default	Specifies that the track is to be enabled if the user's preferences do not indicate that another track would be more appropriate
kind	New	captions chapters descriptions metadata subtitles	Specifies the kind of text track
label	New	*text*	Specifies the title of the text track
src	New	*URL*	Required. Specifies the URL of the track file
srclang	New	*language_code*	Specifies the language of the track text data (required if kind="subtitles")

Example:

```
<html>
<body>
        <video width="320" height="240" controls>
          <source src="forrest_gump.mp4" type="video/mp4">
          <source src="forrest_gump.ogg" type="video/ogg">
          <track src="subtitles_en.vtt" kind="subtitles" srclang="en" label="English">
```

```
    <track src="subtitles_no.vtt" kind="subtitles" srclang="no" label="Norwegian">
   </video>
</body>
</html>
```

3 New Form Elements

Tag	Description
<datalist>	Specifies a list of pre-defined options for input controls
<keygen>	Defines a key-pair generator field (for forms)
<output>	Defines the result of a calculation

3.1 <datalist> tag

❖ **Definition and Usage**

- The <datalist> tag specifies a list of pre-defined options for an <input> element.
- The <datalist> tag is used to provide an "autocomplete" feature on <input> elements. Users will see a drop-down list of pre-defined options as they input data.
- Use the <input> element's list attribute to bind it together with a <datalist> element.

Example:

```
<html>
<body>
        <form action="demo_form.asp" method="get">
        <input list="browsers" name="browser">
        <datalist id="browsers">
          <option value="Internet Explorer">
```


Prof. Nitin Chikani
Atmiya Institute Of Technology & Sci. Rajkot, India

```
    <option value="Firefox">
    <option value="Chrome">
    <option value="Opera">
    <option value="Safari">
  </datalist>
  <input type="submit">
  </form>
  <p><strong>Note :< /strong> the datalist tag is not supported in Internet Explorer
  9 and earlier versions, or in Safari. </p>
</body>
</html>
```

Output:

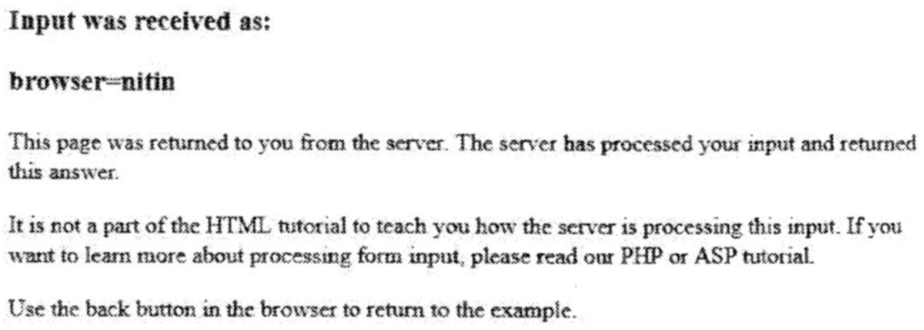

nitin | Submit Query

Note: The datalist tag is not supported in Internet Explorer 9 and earlier versions, or in Safari.

Input was received as:

browser=nitin

This page was returned to you from the server. The server has processed your input and returned this answer.

It is not a part of the HTML tutorial to teach you how the server is processing this input. If you want to learn more about processing form input, please read our PHP or ASP tutorial.

Use the back button in the browser to return to the example.

3.2 <keygen> tag

- **Definition and Usage**

- The <keygen> tag specifies a key-pair generator field used for forms.

Prof. Nitin Chikani
Atmiya Institute Of Technology & Sci. Rajkot, India

- When the form is submitted, the private key is stored locally, and the public key is sent to the server.

❖ **Attributes:**

New : New in HTML5.

Attribute		Value	Description
autofocus	New	autofocus	Specifies that a <keygen> element should automatically get focus when the page loads
challenge	New	challenge	Specifies that the value of the <keygen> element should be challenged when submitted
disabled	New	disabled	Specifies that a <keygen> element should be disabled
form	New	*form_id*	Specifies one or more forms the <keygen> element belongs to
keytype	New	rsa dsa ec	Specifies the security algorithm of the key
name	New	*name*	Defines a name for the <keygen> element

Example:

```
<html>
<body>
        <form action="demo_keygen.asp" method="get">
          Username: <input type="text" name="usr_name">
          Encryption: <keygen name="security">
          <input type="submit">
        </form>
        <p><strong>Note:</strong> The keygen tag is not supported in Internet
        Explorer.</p>
</body>
</html>
```

Output:

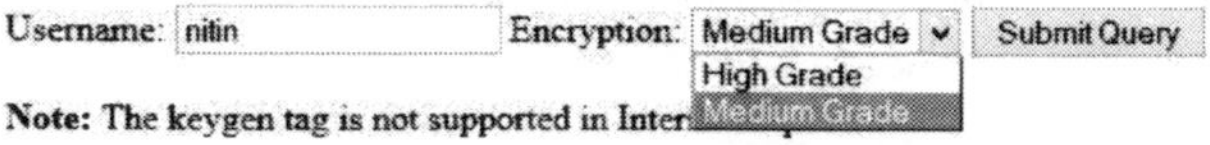

Username: nitin Encryption: Medium Grade Submit Query
High Grade
Medium Grade

Note: The keygen tag is not supported in Inter

Input was received as:

**usr_name=nitin&security=MIIBOjCBpDCBnzANBgkq
hkiG9w0BAQEFAAOBjQAwgYkCgYEArLOPEDdaLz
M%2BQHLd%0D%0Aom%2B9MSgm6zMs3%2B09q
7bvFUtyUx5KPxKfa0kqIaVCmlyFfluInrA1zgDqj2Pfk
qwv%0D%0Ahi%2BucW5VTInDcNh11yLJnxRsI%2B
9rN5U5iy8lbM%2F9xN7f4jBjU7a7MSA89NoqV8DU%
0D%0ALyqd1HhikgU2wzK3FOgCt5pIPKMCAwEAA
RYAMA0GCSqGSIb3DQEBBAUAA4GBAIkz%0D%0
AzY0XnUa1a%2BzB9VSRIAyZv0Ov%2FJtg2zsb0dpi
kBGSNiEMUqKxEgyOUEc211sMYpRl%0D%0AsA1V
kJdN6%2B%2Fnh3%2FMgb4iZFi4y4PcMj24pg7Fv9r
kDhbdmZFWyiTVFGeHPhbOh2%2B3%0D%0ABx5
mBaeedE5VnNiDtqv3y7E%2B%2FzO2bEnd1C6lb05P**

This page was returned to you from the server. The server has processed your input and returned this answer.

It is not a part of the HTML5 tutorial to teach you how the server is processing this input. If you want to learn more about processing form input, please read our PHP or ASP tutorial.

Use the back button in the browser to return to the example.

3.3 <output> tag

❖ Definition and Usage

➢ The <output> tag represents the result of a calculation (like one performed by a script).

❖ Attributes:

New : New in HTML5.

Attribute	Value	Description
for New	*element_id*	Specifies the relationship between the result of the calculation, and the elements used in the calculation
form New	*form_id*	Specifies one or more forms the output element belongs to
name New	*name*	Specifies a name for the output element

Prof. Nitin Chikani
Atmiya Institute Of Technology & Sci. Rajkot, India

Example:

```
<html>
<body>
    <form oninput="x.value=parseInt(a.value)+parseInt(b.value)">0
    <input type="range" id="a" value="50">100
    +<input type="number" id="b" value="50">
    =<output name="x" for="a b"></output>
    </form>
    <p><strong>Note:</strong> The output tag is not supported in Internet
    Explorer.</p>
</body>
</html>
```

Output:

0 100 + 50 =116

Note: The output tag is not supported in Internet Explorer.

- **HTML5 New Form Attributes**

- **New attributes for <form>:**

1. autocomplete
2. novalidate

- **New attributes for <input>:**

1. autocomplete
2. autofocus
3. form
4. formaction

5. formenctype
6. formmethod
7. formnovalidate
8. formtarget
9. height and width
10. list
11. min and max
12. multiple
13. pattern (regexp)
14. placeholder
15. required
16. step

4.1.1<form> / <input> autocomplete Attribute

- The autocomplete attribute specifics whether a form or input field should have autocomplete on or off.
- When autocomplete is on, the browser automatically complete values based on values that the user has entered before.

Example:

```
<html>
<body>
        <form action="demo_form.asp" autocomplete="on">
          First name:<input type="text" name="fname"><br>
          Last name: <input type="text" name="lname"><br>
          E-mail: <input type="email" name="email" autocomplete="off"><br>
          <input type="submit">
```

```
    </form>
    <p>Fill in and submit the form, then reload the page to see how autocomplete works.</p>
    <p>Notice that autocomplete is "on" for the form, but "off" for the e-mail field.</p>
</body>
</html>
```

Output:

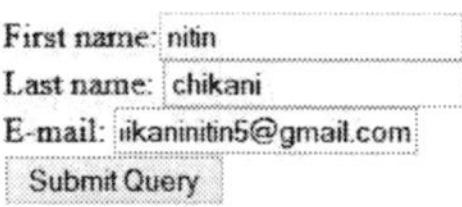

Fill in and submit the form, then reload the page to see how autocomplete works.

Notice that autocomplete is "on" for the form, but "off" for the e-mail field.

Input was received as:

fname=nitin&lname=chikani&email=chikaninitin5%40gmail.com

This page was returned to you from the server. The server has processed your input and returned this answer.

It is not a part of the HTML5 tutorial to teach you how the server is processing this input. If you want to learn more about processing form input, please read our PHP or ASP tutorial.

Use the back button in the browser to return to the example.

4.1.2<form> novalidate Attribute

- The novalidate attribute is a Boolean attribute.
- When present, it specifies that the form-data (input) should not be validated when submitted.

Example:

```
<html>
<body>
```


Prof. Nitin Chikani
Atmiya Institute Of Technology & Sci. Rajkot, India

```
        <form action="demo_form.asp" novalidate>
        E-mail: <input type="email" name="user_email">
        <input type="submit">
        </form>
        <p><strong>Note:</strong> The novalidate attribute of the form tag is not
        supported in Internet Explorer 9 and earlier versions, or in Safari.</p>
</body>
</html>
```

Output:

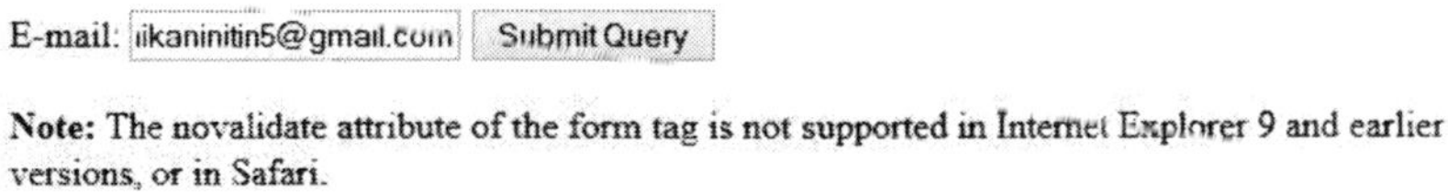
E-mail: iikaninitin5@gmail.com
Submit Query
Note: The novalidate attribute of the form tag is not supported in Internet Explorer 9 and earlier versions, or in Safari.

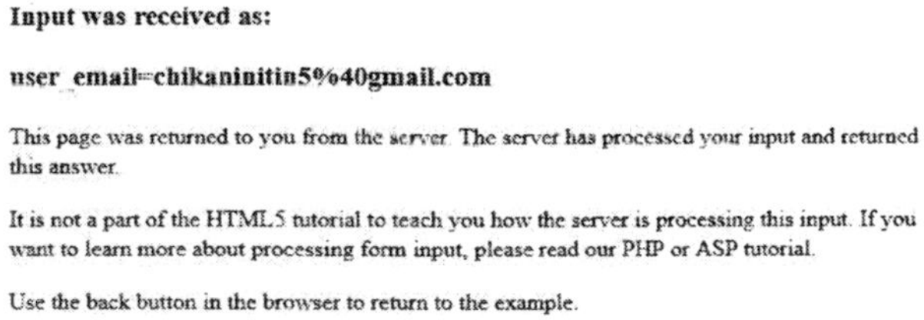
Input was received as:
user_email=chikaninitin5%40gmail.com
This page was returned to you from the server. The server has processed your input and returned this answer.
It is not a part of the HTML5 tutorial to teach you how the server is processing this input. If you want to learn more about processing form input, please read our PHP or ASP tutorial.
Use the back button in the browser to return to the example.

4.2.2<input> autofocus Attribute

- The autofocus attribute is a boolean attribute.
- When present, it specifies that an <input> element should automatically get focus when the page loads.

Example:

```
<html>
<body>
        <form action="demo_form.html">
```


Prof. Nitin Chikani
Atmiya Institute Of Technology & Sci. Rajkot, India

```
    First name:<input type="text" name="fname" autofocus><br>
    Last name: <input type="text" name="lname"><br>
    <input type="submit">
  </form>
  <p><strong>Note:</strong> The autofocus attribute of the input tag is not
  supported in Internet Explorer 9 and earlier versions.</p>
</body>
</html>
```

Output:

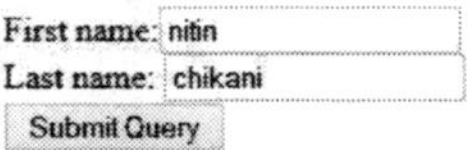

Note: The autofocus attribute of the input tag is not supported in Internet Explorer 9 and earlier versions.

4.2.3 <input> form Attribute

- The form attribute specifies one or more forms an <input> element belongs to.

Example:

```
<html>
<body>
  <form action="demo_form.html" id="form1">
  First name: <input type="text" name="fname"><br>
  <input type="submit" value="Submit">
  </form>
  <p>The "Last name" field below is outside the form element, but still part of the
  form.</p>
  Last name: <input type="text" name="lname" form="form1">
```


Prof. Nitin Chikani
Atmiya Institute Of Technology & Sci. Rajkot, India

```
</body>
</html>
```

Output:

First name: nitin
Submit

The "Last name" field below is outside the form element, but still part of the form.

Last name: chikani

4.2.4 <input> formaction Attribute

- The formaction attribute specifies the URL of a file that will process the input control when the form is submitted.
- The formaction attribute overrides the action attribute of the <form> element.

Example:

```
<html>
<body>
    <form action="demo_form.html">
      First name: <input type="text" name="fname"><br>
      Last name: <input type="text" name="lname"><br>
      <input type="submit" value="Submit"><br>
      <input type="submit" formaction="demo_admin.asp" value="Submit as
    admin">
    </form>
    <p><strong>Note:</strong> The formaction attribute of the input tag is not
    supported in Internet Explorer 9 and earlier versions.</p>
</body>
</html>
```

Output:

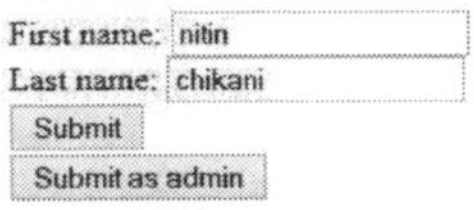

Note: The formaction attribute of the input tag is not supported in Internet Explorer 9 and earlier versions.

Admin page

Input was received as: fname=nitin&lname=chikani

This page was returned to you from the server. The server has processed your input and returned this answer.

It is not a part of the HTML tutorial to teach you how the server is processing this input. If you want to learn more about processing form input, please read our PHP or ASP tutorial.

Use the back button in the browser to return to the example.

4.2.5 <input> formenctype Attribute

- The formenctype attribute specifies how the form-data should be encoded when submitting it to the server (only for forms with method="post")
- The formenctype attribute overrides the enctype attribute of the <form> element.

Example:

```
<html>
<body>
    <form action="demo_post_enctype.html" method="post">
     First name: <input type="text" name="fname"><br>
     <input type="submit" value="Submit">
     <input type="submit" formenctype="multipart/form-data" value="Submit as
       Multipart/form-data">
    </form>
    <p><strong>Note:</strong> The formenctype attribute of the input tag is not
    supported in Internet Explorer 9 and earlier versions.</p>
```

```
</body>
</html>
```

Output:

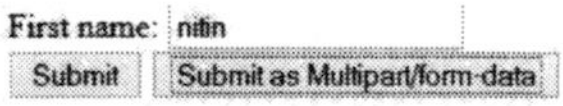

First name: nitin

Submit | Submit as Multipart/form-data

Note: The formenctype attribute of the input tag is not supported in Internet Explorer 9 and earlier versions.

Input was received as:

-----------------------------138952236217085 Content-Disposition: form-data; name="fname" nitin -----------------------------138952236217085--

This page was returned to you from the server. The server has processed your input and returned this answer.

It is not a part of the HTML5 tutorial to teach you how the server is processing this input. If you want to learn more about processing form input, please read our PHP or ASP tutorial.

Use the back button in the browser to return to the example.

4.2.6 <input> formmethod Attribute

- The formmethod attribute defines the HTTP method for sending form-data to the action URL.
- The formmethod attribute overrides the method attribute of the <form> element.

Example:

```
<html>
<body>
    <form action="demo_form.html" method="get">
      First name: <input type="text" name="fname"><br>
      Last name: <input type="text" name="lname"><br>
      <input type="submit" value="Submit">
```


Prof. Nitin Chikani
Atmiya Institute Of Technology & Sci. Rajkot, India

```
    <input type="submit" formmethod="post" formaction="demo_post.html"
    value="Submit using POST">
    </form>
    <p><strong>Note:</strong> The formmethod attribute of the input tag is not
    supported in Internet Explorer 9 and earlier versions.</p>
</body>
</html>
```

Output:

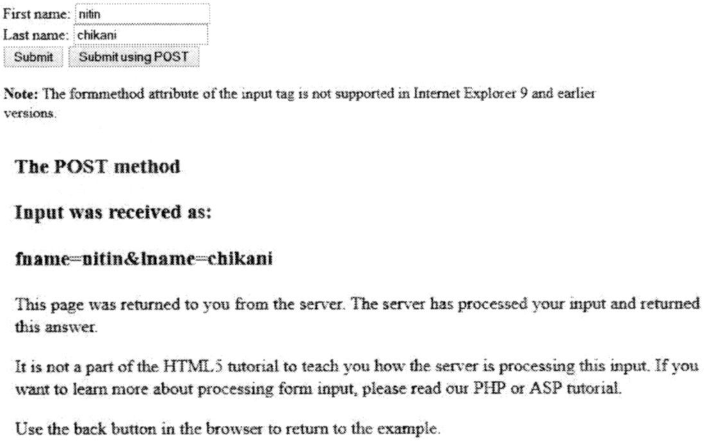

First name: nitin
Last name: chikani
Submit | Submit using POST

Note: The formmethod attribute of the input tag is not supported in Internet Explorer 9 and earlier versions.

The POST method

Input was received as:

fname=nitin&lname=chikani

This page was returned to you from the server. The server has processed your input and returned this answer.

It is not a part of the HTML5 tutorial to teach you how the server is processing this input. If you want to learn more about processing form input, please read our PHP or ASP tutorial.

Use the back button in the browser to return to the example.

4.2.7 <input> formnovalidate Attribute

- The novalidate attribute is a boolean attribute.
- When present, it specifies that the <input> element should not be validated when submitted.
- The formnovalidate attribute overrides the novalidate attribute of the <form> element.

Example:

```
<html>
<body>
        <form action="demo_form.html">
          E-mail: <input type="email" name="userid"><br>
          <input type="submit" value="Submit"><br>
          <input type="submit" formnovalidate value="Submit without validation">
        </form>
        <p><strong>Note:</strong> The formnovalidate attribute of the input tag is not
        supported in Internet Explorer 9 and earlier versions, or in Safari.</p>
</body>
</html>
```

Output:

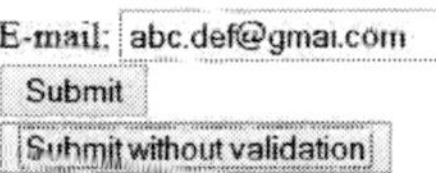

Note: The formnovalidate attribute of the input tag is not supported in Internet Explorer 9 and earlier versions, or in Safari.

Input was received as:

userid=abc.def%40gmai.com

This page was returned to you from the server. The server has processed your input and returned this answer.

It is not a part of the HTML5 tutorial to teach you how the server is processing this input. If you want to learn more about processing form input, please read our PHP or ASP tutorial.

Use the back button in the browser to return to the example.

4.2.8 <input> formtarget Attribute

- The formtarget attribute specifies a name or a keyword that indicates where to display the response that is received after submitting the form.

- The formtarget attribute overrides the target attribute of the <form> element.

Example:

```
<html>
<body>
        <form action="demo_form.html">
          First name: <input type="text" name="fname"><br>
          Last name: <input type="text" name="lname"><br>
          <input type="submit" value="Submit as normal">
          <input type="submit" formtarget="_blank" value="Submit to a new
        window/tab">
        </form>
        <p><strong>Note:</strong> The formtarget attribute of the input tag is not
        supported in Internet Explorer 9 and earlier versions.</p>
</body>
</html>
```

Output:

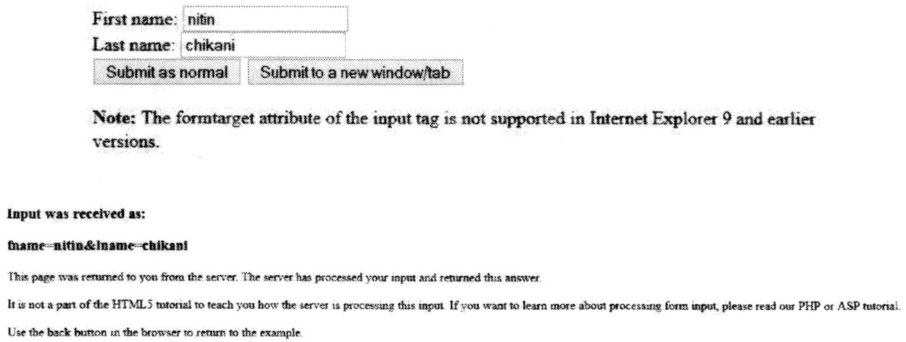

First name: nitin
Last name: chikani
Submit as normal | Submit to a new window/tab

Note: The formtarget attribute of the input tag is not supported in Internet Explorer 9 and earlier versions.

Input was received as:

fname=nitin&lname=chikani

This page was returned to you from the server. The server has processed your input and returned this answer.

It is not a part of the HTML5 tutorial to teach you how the server is processing this input. If you want to learn more about processing form input, please read our PHP or ASP tutorial.

Use the back button in the browser to return to the example.

Prof. Nitin Chikani
Atmiya Institute Of Technology & Sci. Rajkot, India

4.2.9 <input> height and width Attributes

- The height and width attributes specify the height and width of an <input> element.

Note: The height and width attributes are only used with <input type="image">.

Example:

```
<html>
<body>
        <form action="demo_form.html">
          First name: <input type="text" name="fname"><br>
          Last name: <input type="text" name="lname"><br>
          <input type="image" src="img_submit.gif" alt="Submit" width="48"
        height="48">
        </form>
        <p><b>Note:</b> The input type="image" sends the X and Y coordinates of the
        click that activated the image button.</p>
</body>
</html>
```

Output:

First name: nitin
Last name: chikani

Note: The input type="image" sends the X and Y coordinates of the click that activated the image button.

Prof. Nitin Chikani
Atmiya Institute Of Technology & Sci. Rajkot, India

4.2.10 <input> list Attribute

- The list attribute refers to a <datalist> element that contains pre-defined options for an <input> element.

Example:

```
<html>
<body>
        <form action="demo_form.html" method="get">
        <input list="browsers" name="browser">
        <datalist id="browsers">
          <option value="Internet Explorer">
          <option value="Firefox">
          <option value="Chrome">
          <option value="Opera">
          <option value="Safari">
        </datalist>
        <input type="submit">
        </form>
        <p><b>Note:</b> The datalist tag is not supported in Internet Explorer 9 and
        earlier versions, or in Safari.</p>
</body>
</html>
```

Output:

Note: The datalist tag is not supported in Internet Explorer 9 and earlier versions, or in Safari.

Prof. Nitin Chikani
Atmiya Institute Of Technology & Sci. Rajkot, India

4.2.11 <input> min and max Attributes

- The min and max attributes specify the minimum and maximum value for an <input> element.

Note: The min and max attributes works with the following input types: number, range, date, datetime, datetime-local, month, time and week.

Example:

```
<html>
<body>
        <form action="demo_form.html">
          Enter a date before 1980-01-01:
          <input type="date" name="bday" max="1979-12-31"><br>
          Enter a date after 2000-01-01:
          <input type="date" name="bday" min="2000-01-02"><br>
          Quantity (between 1 and 5):
          <input type="number" name="quantity" min="1" max="5"><br>
          <input type="submit">
          </form>
</body>
</html>
```

Output:

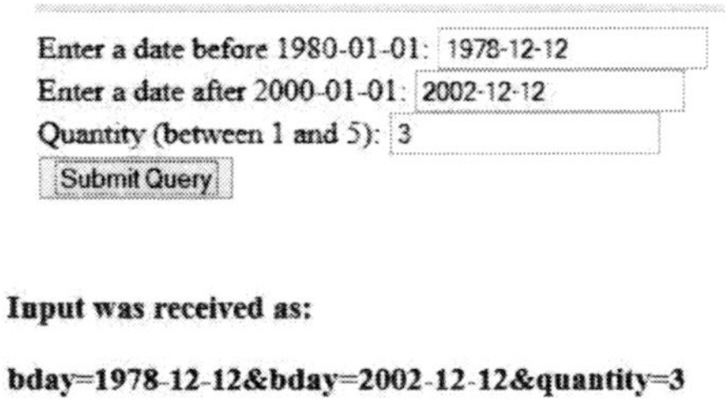

Enter a date before 1980-01-01: 1978-12-12
Enter a date after 2000-01-01: 2002-12-12
Quantity (between 1 and 5): 3
Submit Query

Input was received as:

bday=1978-12-12&bday=2002-12-12&quantity=3

Prof. Nitin Chikani
Atmiya Institute Of Technology & Sci. Rajkot, India

4.2.12 <input> multiple Attribute

- The multiple attribute is a boolean attribute.
- When present, it specifies that the user is allowed to enter more than one value in the <input> element.

Note: The multiple attribute works with the following input types: email, and file.

Example:

```
<html>
<body>
        <form action="demo_form.html">
          Select images: <input type="file" name="img" multiple>
          <input type="submit">
        </form>
</body>
</html>
```

Output:

Select images: Browse.. No files selected. Submit Query

4.2.13 <input> pattern Attribute

- The pattern attribute specifies a regular expression that the <input> element's value is checked against.

Note: The pattern attribute works with the following input types: text, search, url, tel, email, and password.

Example:

```
<html>
<body>
        <form action="demo_form.html">
```


Prof. Nitin Chikani
Atmiya Institute Of Technology & Sci. Rajkot, India

```
    Country code: <input type="text" name="country_code" pattern="[A-Za-z]{3}"
    title="Three letter country code">
    <input type="submit">
    </form>
</body>
</html>
```

Output:

Country code: 202 Submit Query

Please match the requested format: Three letter country code.

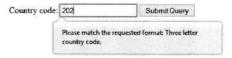

4.2.14 <input> placeholder Attribute

- The placeholder attribute specifies a short hint that describes the expected value of an input field (e.g. a sample value or a short description of the expected format).
- The short hint is displayed in the input field before the user enters a value.

Example:

```
<html>
<body>
    <form action="demo_form.html">
     <input type="text" name="fname" placeholder="First name"><br>
     <input type="text" name="lname" placeholder="Last name"><br>
     <input type="submit" value="Submit">
    </form>
</body>
</html>
```

Output:

Prof. Nitin Chikani
Atmiya Institute Of Technology & Sci. Rajkot, India

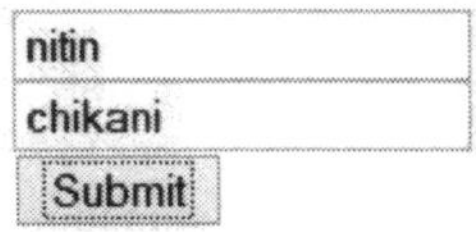

4.2.15 <input> step Attribute

- The step attribute specifies the legal number intervals for an <input> element.
- Example: if step="3", legal numbers could be -3, 0, 3, 6, etc.

Note: The step attribute works with the following input types: number, range, date, datetime, datetime-local, month, time and week.

Example:

```
<html>
<body>
        <form action="demo_form.html">
          <input type="number" name="points" step="3">
          <input type="submit">
        </form>
</body>
</html>
```

Output:

Input was received as:

123 Submit Query **points=123**

4.2.16 <input> step Attribute

- The step attribute specifies the legal number intervals for an <input> element.
- Example: if step="3", legal numbers could be -3, 0, 3, 6, etc.

Note: The step attribute works with the following input types: number, range, date, datetime, datetime-local, month, time and week.

Prof. Nitin Chikani
Atmiya Institute Of Technology & Sci. Rajkot, India

Example:

```
<html>
<body>
    <form action="demo_form.html">
      <input type="number" name="points" step="3">
      <input type="submit">
    </form>
</body>
</html>
```

Output:

hi | Submit Query

Input was received as:

points=hi

HTML5 Web Storage

What is HTML5 Web Storage?

- With HTML5, web pages can store data locally within the user's browser.
- Earlier, this was done with cookies. However, Web Storage is more secure and faster. The data is not included with every server request, but used ONLY when asked for. It is also possible to store large amounts of data, without affecting the website's performance.
- The data is stored in key/value pairs, and a web page can only access data stored by itself.

Two new objects for storing data on the client:

1. localStorage - stores data with no expiration date
2. sessionStorage - stores data for one session

1. The localStorage Object

- The localStorage object stores the data with no expiration date. The data will not be deleted when the browser is closed, and will be available the next day, week, or year.

Example:

```
<html>
<body>
        <div id="result"></div>
        <script>
        if(typeof(Storage)!=="undefined")
          {
          localStorage.lastname="Nitin";
          document.getElementById("result").innerHTML="Last name: " +
        localStorage.lastname;
          }
        else
          {
          document.getElementById("result").innerHTML="Sorry, your browser does not
        support web storage...";
          }
        </script>
</body>
</html>
```

Output:

Last name: Nitin

Prof. Nitin Chikani
Atmiya Institute Of Technology & Sci. Rajkot, India

2. The sessionStorage Object

- The sessionStorage object is equal to the localStorage object, **except** that it stores the data for only one session. The data is deleted when the user closes the browser window.

The following example counts the number of times a user has clicked a button, in the current session:

Example:

```
<html>
<head>
        <script>
        function clickCounter()
        {
        if(typeof(Storage)!=="undefined")
          {
          if (sessionStorage.clickcount)
            {
            sessionStorage.clickcount=Number(sessionStorage.clickcount)+1;
            }
          else
            {
            sessionStorage.clickcount=1;
            }
          document.getElementById("result").innerHTML="You have clicked the button
        " + sessionStorage.clickcount + " time(s) in this session.";
          }
```


Prof. Nitin Chikani
Atmiya Institute Of Technology & Sci. Rajkot, India

```
        else
         {
         document.getElementById("result").innerHTML="Sorry, your browser does not
        support web storage...";
         }
        }
        </script>
</head>
<body>
        <p><button onclick="clickCounter()" type="button">Click me!</button></p>
        <div id="result"></div>
        <p>Click the button to see the counter increase.</p>
        <p>Close the browser tab (or window), and try again, and the counter is
        reset.</p>
</body>
</html>
```

Output:

Click me!

You have clicked the button 4 time(s) in this session.

Click the button to see the counter increase.

Close the browser tab (or window), and try again, and the counter is reset.

References:

http://www.w3schools.com

http://www.google.com/

Prof. Nitin Chikani
Atmiya Institute Of Technology & Sci. Rajkot, India

Lightning Source UK Ltd.
Milton Keynes UK
UKOW02f0202260815

257499UK00002B/112/P